Game Changer

David M Rothbart

Dedication

This book is dedicated to my wife Janet, our children, grandchildren, family and friends. I could not have made it through this medical crisis without their love and support.

Table of Contents

ISBN-13:978-1533121943

Introduction

Each of us will, at some point in our lives, experience a Game Changer. This could come in the form of catastrophic illness, trauma (physical or mental) or a life ending event. Other than end of life the Game Changer is a circumstance(s) that we over time may have the ability to recover from. My Game Changer was physical and mental caused by a catastrophic medical event that literally blindsided me and brought me to a near death experience. It has been a number of months and although I have made great strides, I am still working on my recovery process both physical and mental.

When you are faced with the Game Changer your life takes a number of turns that in most instances, one is not prepared for. If you are capable, you first might ask, "what is happening to me?" You then move on to the discovery period of, "how am I and other professionals going to deal with my circumstances?" With time and healing, you may get a sense of recovery. I think that for me it was the most terrifying confluence of the Game Changer. What was my future going to look like? Will I be able to take care of myself, walk again, feed myself, have a productive and active life with myself, my wife, family and friends. These are all scary thoughts which are all part of the Game Changer.

We will all handle or have difficulty handling the Game Changer based on our mental and physical status at the time. From my experience I believe that the more awake and aware you are, at the time, the more difficult the event and/or series of events will be to wrap your arms around. For me, having a systemic infection, stroke and heart valve deterioration there were many parts of my experience that are clouded. I had an overall feeling of drifting. I went from one medical test to another with the attitude of "oh well, whatever". I remember not having a feeling of possible impending disaster. Looking back, it was most likely my body's defense mechanism taking over creating internal calmness. Being close to death my mind may have been in preparation mode in the event that I didn't make it.

As time marches on I find that the events of my Game Changer are growing dimmer as my memory of events fades. My mind is slowly letting go of the catastrophic events that nearly obliterated my existence. I call that moving on, the catharsis I need to open up my being once again to the gift of life.

The Onset

In October 2015 we arrived home from a two-week vacation with my wife, sister and brother-in-law and friends in the wine country of Paso Robles, CA and weeklong coastal California cruise. What a glorious time we had. The trip, weather, company and my health were excellent (or so I thought). Three days after our return the shit hit the fan. Prior to that I had experienced good health during my 64 years having only surgery to remove my tonsils removal when I was five. It was quite a long tenure without medical problems. Yes, I had my share of accidental injuries along with broken bones, bruises and sprains but nothing that disrupted my life to any great extent.

On October 18, 2015 I woke up to the beginning of the Game Changer. When I opened my eyes that morning I had a great deal of difficulty getting out of bed. My left hip and leg were in severe pain. I expressed my extreme discomfort to my wife Janet and did my best to get out of bed and begin my day. After several days of enduring pain and increasing difficulty walking I decided to get some chiropractic treatment thinking that my malady was orthopedic in nature. So off to the chiropractor I went. He performed an examination and determined that there were some issues in my lower spine and hip area that needed adjustment and so I began treatment. Without blood tests, which were not performed, there was no way for him to know of the infection that was invading my body. After three weeks I was not seeing or feeling any appreciable improvement. My chiropractor recommended I see the acupuncturist in his office. Once again, after several treatments, no improvement. Surprisingly the thought of, "what the hell is happening to me?", did not cross my mind.

I started to notice that my brain was telling me to go and my body was saying no. It would take me what seemed like forever to get up from a sitting position or to start walking from a standstill. Obviously something physically was very wrong. I was spending all day, every day, for the next few weeks sitting or lying around the house with increasing mental despondence. In addition, I was experiencing swelling and significant discomfort in my hands which was preventing me from performing many functional tasks.

On December 1st, Janet emphatically suggested (more like insisted) that I see the family doctor for an evaluation of my worsening condition. So off to the family physician I went. You have to understand, I was not a fan of doctors and had not seen one in quite a long time. I had been in the habit of Googling and self-medicating to provide care on my own. In hindsight, it was not a very good strategy.

After a brief examination the doctor told me that he suspected a rheumatoid issue and had me go for blood studies. I was definitely starting to fade mentally and do not have a great recollection of the doctor or lab visit. Now in hindsight, it was apparent that I was on a rapid downhill slide.

I don't remember much of the rest of that day or evening. The next day Janet was taking our grandson to see Sesame Street Live and being in the compromised state of health that I was staying home was my only option, on the couch, covered with a blanket. That is really the last thing I remember. I have no recollection of moving off of the couch although I have been told that I ate lunch and called the doctor's office to see if the lab results had come in. I had become oblivious to my surroundings and seriously declining state of health.

Saint Mary's Admission

By December 2nd, I had become completely delirious, combative and irrational. My illness was invading my body with a vengeance. Janet called the doctor and was told to take me to the emergency room. I vaguely remember still being at the house and ranting about how I was not going to the hospital and how I wanted a pow wow meeting with our two sons. I told Janet that I hated her and this whole thing was a conspiracy. My toxic brain was in full gear. She told me that if I did not get in the car she was going to call 911 for paramedic assistance and that she did not want to wake up next to a corpse in the morning (I am not sure that she actually realized how on the mark she was as I was literally near death). I reluctantly got in the car with no recollection of the drive to Saint Mary's ER. When we arrived I was taken into a treatment room and my game changing life altering adventure began.

I was admitted into the ER with a primary diagnosis of severe sepsis with strep agalacticae bacteremia, toxic metabolic encephalopathy and a stroke cause by emboli to my brain. I was not a bundle of joy in the ER treatment room. After being hooked up to a number of IV's, which included medication to hydrate as well as antibiotics, I decided I was leaving. Security was called and two rather large officers made sure that I stayed put. That was the start of a six day stay at Saint Mary's completely NPO (nothing by mouth) for what seemed like endless invasive and non-invasive testing. If you have never been NPO for a week I have to tell you, it is hell. I was being hydrated and fed by an IV. My mouth felt like a mountain of cotton balls and dry undershirts were stuffed in it. The best the nursing staff could come up with for me was moist cotton swabs. At that point I would have settled for burnt toast and water. I was visited and probed by what seemed like a never ending parade of physicians, medical residents, PA's and nurse's day and night for my entire stay. Match that with a plethora of gurney rides to x-ray, CT, MRI and cardiac testing along with more blood tests than I had blood to give and you were on my daily ride for the next six days. Surprisingly I was calm and almost oblivious to my medical encounters even when one of the medical residents came into my room and inappropriately informed me the odds were very good for me to lose my battle for life. I have to preface my lament by saying that the staff was nothing less than fantastic, extremely professional and attentive.

As the days progressed my physical condition continued to deteriorate. Not moving much for the better part of a month was showing its effect on my body and mind. Muscle deterioration was happening at a rapid rate. I no longer had control of my lower body and no ability to walk. My non ambulatory condition was more troubling to me than the grave illness I was battling. Not having the ability to move is pretty scary. It seemed that no matter how hard I tried I could not move my legs or torso. The feeling was like being trapped in your own body. I can vaguely remember the parade of people coming in and out of my room. I was asked, daily, what day, month and year it was. My answer was always the same, "I have no idea".

On December 6th a Transesophageal Echocardiogram was performed (TEE). I was mildly sedated and my throat and esophagus were numbed. An electronic probe was passed down my throat and the test began. I actually felt quite calm during the procedure. What was revealed from the test was the icing on the cake. The cardiologist discovered that my mitral valve had been eaten away by the infection that had invaded my body. He said the valve was completely destroyed and pieces were breaking off with every beat of my heart. It was determined that I was going to need open heart surgery to replace the valve and I was transferred from Saint Mary's to Meijer Heart Center in Grand Rapids, MI. Fortunately for me, Meijer Heart has a reputation for being one of the top heart institutes in the country and a premier center in the Mid-West. I was loaded into an ambulance and on my way for the short ride to Meijer Heart across town. I have to say, if I was out of it mentally before the ride I was fully awake during the transport. From the time I was transferred from my hospital bed to the stretcher I was bounced around like a sack of potatoes in the back of a pickup truck. I am not totally sure what the deal was. I was admitted to Meijer Heart in the cardiac intensive care unit and ready to begin the next phase of my journey.

Meijer Heart Center

Being in a heart center with a top reputation in the nation was a blessing for me certainly a good step in the right direction for saving my life. Had I been treated in a facility not as well equipped and staffed with highly skilled medical personnel I would not be here to write this journal. During my stay at the heart center Janet kept a journal to keep our concerned family, friends and acquaintances informed about my condition.

Janet's journal entry December 7th:

Just wanted to let you know that David is in the hospital. He is one lucky guy. After our Paso Robles wine visit and Pacific Coast cruise late in September into October, he developed a low back issue. Went to the chiropractor and acupuncturist for several weeks of treatment but it did not help. He became confused and began speaking gibberish. I brought him to the emergency room and he was admitted with sepsis in his bloodstream. He has a psoas muscle abscess in his hip area. They found that he has Endocarditis with growth on the mitral valve and it is mostly torn and flapping. He is going to have a cardiac catheterization in the morning and they are trying to determine, infection-wise, the best time to schedule him for open heart surgery.

I am still pretty out of it with very sporadic recollection of my surroundings and condition. For some reason I do not remember any fear or anxiety regarding my condition or my upcoming open heart surgery. Maybe it was my mind's way of shutting the trauma down. The endless invasive and non-invasive tests continued without regard to time of day. I have some memory of being wheeled out of my room during the day and evening for one test or another. Most likely this was done as a part of facility scheduling. I was in the cardiac intensive care unit where I was being monitored 24/7.

Unable to move, all of my physical needs were taken care of by the attentive staff. I remember that no matter how hard I tried I could not move my legs or my body so whatever position I was placed in, there I stayed until I was repositioned to prevent bed sores.

Janet's journal entry December 8th:

The cardiac surgeon came by today. He said that they were going to hold off on the valve replacement surgery until sometime next week. He said if there is any infection anywhere in David's system there is a greater chance it would infect the new valves and it would kill him.

This is not exactly what Janet wanted to hear and when she conveyed that information to me I had little reaction. I was resigned to the fact that I was caught up in the waiting game. Meanwhile my condition was worsening with congestive heart failure setting in. My body was swollen, I was NPO, still not allowed to eat anything, I was unable to move, but still in spite of it all I was amazingly calm and detached. I was, however, becoming extremely depressed.

Janet's journal entry December 9th:

David is depressed. I explained to him that the wait is best for him so they can treat him with more antibiotics. His mitral valve is not working and backwashing into his lungs causing tachycardia.

Not being mobile I was not particularly breathless and was not experiencing any heart pain. I am sure that the sedative and other medication being pumped into me from numerous IV's was counteracting my deteriorating but stable condition. The testing continued along with the endless parade of physicians, PA's, nurses, medical residents and aids continued, catering to my every need. I was a rock star on grand rounds each day. I can remember hearing that my case was very unique and most likely was a great educational tool.

Janet's journal entry December 10th:

Drains were placed in David's lungs so his heart rate would drop as the fluid was relieved. His heart rate is still high. His blood pressure is low so they are giving him IV

albumin. His temp is normal. They have re-cultured his
leg from the drains and put new drains into the area
where he had the abscess and those results are pending.
They just did another echocardiogram which showed that
in addition to the damaged Mitral valve he has an infected
Aortic valve. Waiting anxiously for his surgery to be
scheduled as he will need two valves replaced. Cardiac
meds are keeping him stable. They are watching him
closely and giving him pain meds to keep him comfortable.
As long as he is stable his doctors want the antibiotics
working in him for as long as possible. Poor guy is hungry,
but they won't feed him in the event his vitals crash and
they are forced to do the surgery.

My medical crisis is really taking a toll on Janet, our
sons and daughter-in-law. I am sure that they are tired
and scared of what my possible unfortunate outcome
could be. Our sons Scott and Dustin, along with Janet, our
daughter-in-law Jocelyn, and our grandsons have been at
my bedside holding a vigil until my surgery. Scott is a
scientist at the Van Andel Research Institute, which is
adjacent to Meijer Heart Center. He was able to speak
frequently to my doctors and get a clinical account of my
condition and what is in store for me. This is very helpful
to Janet and the rest of the family to keep them abreast of
my medical status. For the most part, I am so out of it
that I do not remember any of them being there but I

know that their presence and loving energy was moving me forward.

Janet's journal entry December 14th:

Surgery is on schedule for today. Definitely the Mitral valve will be replaced. They will scope the inside of his heart before they do surgery to see what extent the Aortic valve is compromised and make the decision whether to replace it at that time. Surgery took 6+ hours and both valves were replaced. David was removed from the heart lung machine and his heart restarted. Valves and heart are working on their own. He is still sedated and on a respirator. Will be at least 6 hours before his is awake and will spend the night in the cardiac recovery unit. He is still not out of the woods. They are watching him closely for bleeds or stroke.

Janet's journal entry December 15th:

He is still on the respirator. He is sedated and being monitored closely. His heart is functioning. The cardiac PA-C just came in. They will possibly reduce his oxygen but will still keep him on the respirator due to pneumonia caused by aspiration after surgery. They will continue X-rays each morning to see how his lungs are clearing. Cardiac meds have been reduced and most likely today they will be discontinued.

Janet's Journal entry December 16th:

Surgery wise all is good. Just need to clear up the lungs.

Janet's journal entry December 17th:

Tested lowering the respirator. Oxygen levels dropped to 89% so they increased the oxygen from 6-8 and set the machine to breathe for him only when needed. He is breathing on his own and they are monitoring him. They will continue to monitor David during the day to see if he is able to keep his oxygen level above 90%. He is still not ready to come off the respirator yet. He has been awake when they tried to lower the oxygen level. He became agitated so they increased his sedation. He knows I am here. Told him I love him and he nodded.

I do not remember anything from the time I was wheeled into the operating room through my six-day sedated time on the respirator. I did have, what seemed to be, an endless stream of not-so-pleasant dreams that I do remember to this day. Prior to my surgery I had extremely vivid floaters in my left eye which were very well defined. Fortunately, they went away after my surgery. The eye doctor told me they were most likely due to the stroke that I had.

Janet's journal entry December 19th:

Happy day - David is weaned off the respirator. He is a bit combative but that will ease up as the sedation wears off. Lot's going on here. Removed from major sedation. Reduced all but one BP medication. Heart is in sinus rhythm and functioning well. If he continues on his own they will disconnect his external pacemaker.

Janet's journal entry December 20th:

David's urinary catheter was removed. Peeing on his own (men, if you have ever had a urinary catheter put in you can testify that it is a miserably uncomfortable procedure. If you have never had one you are blessed and can count your lucky stars. *They put him in a chair and he sat for two hours. He raised each leg while dangling on the side of bed. He is using a breath indicator to exercise his lungs and keep them clear. Plans are to evaluate him for physical therapy. Good chance he will be moved from cardiac intensive care to a regular cardiac unit tomorrow. He is doing good...baby steps.*

At this point I am fully aware of my surroundings. I remember sitting in the chair for the first time and how good it felt. This was the beginning of a very scary time for me with anxiety, depression and thoughts of never being able to walk again.

Yes, I was grateful to be alive and given a second chance but at the same time I was extremely concerned about my future. I cried a lot as it seemed like my emotions were running out of control and questioned Janet about what was in store for me. She told me, along with my doctors, that I would recover and resume a normal life. I was not quite sure what normal meant. Having limited mobility is frightening. No matter how hard I tried mentally I could not get my body to move. Everything required assistance, literally everything. I truly had thoughts of being an invalid, confined to a wheelchair for the rest of my life. When you are confined to the hospital and you cannot tend to even basic functions you quickly lose all of your vanity. I had so many health professionals probing, examining and cleaning every part of my body that modesty quickly went out the window. I really did not care who saw or tended to my naked body, I had bigger fish to fry.

Janet's journal entry December 21st:

The doctor from the thoracic surgical team came in to check David. He said that they'll remove the left chest tube tomorrow. Right is still draining. His heart rate and rhythm are good. They are not using the backup pacemaker any longer. A physical therapy evaluation was ordered. He will probably be moved to 7 cardiac floor tomorrow.

I know that I am on the road to recuperation but feel like I have been in a train wreck. I am still not ambulatory and have little to no ability to move my body even while in bed. The nurses and nursing aids are diligent in keeping my body position adjusted to prevent bed sores and from developing respiratory issues due to my immobility. I am positioned on my back or whatever configuration I am placed in I and I stay that way until I am moved again. One night I awoke to find I was swaddled like an infant, which totally freaked me out. My arms were pinned under the blanket against my sides making it impossible to reach my call button. I had no other choice but to yell for assistance. I asked them to please never do that to me again.

Getting out of bed to move me to a chair is a major ordeal. It takes two people to lift me from the bed to a walker and move another one or two steps to sit down. It was extremely difficult to get my body and legs to work. It was scary and frustrating to say the least. I have had several physical therapy sessions and consider it a great thing to be able to stand, holding the walker, and move two or three feet from the side of the bed to the foot of the bed with assistance. My legs mostly drag on the floor as I attempt to move forward. I am so tired and feel like I have no strength to lift my legs which feel like the weight of torpedoes.

Janet's journal entry December, 22nd:

The thoracic surgeon came in and told David that it is normal for him to feel like he was run over by a truck. He got a good pep talk although I am not sure how much it helped. He seems pretty depressed and crie's a lot. He is still being given Lasix but is not able to empty his bladder fully. It is really difficult to pee lying in bed with a urinal. They decided to put the urinary catheter back in again. David is completely bummed about this medical decision.

When they told me that the catheter was going back in I had a fit. Enough is enough, I am being beaten into submission and just want to be left alone. How much more can I take and why am I being tested has crossed my mind many times. I am starting to wonder if my medical circumstances are the result of some bad karma. Why do bad things happen to good people? My minister, on visits to my hospital bed, assured me that I am not being punished and that karma is not a reason for my condition. Positive thoughts, prayers and messages of good will[definitely moved me in the right direction of recovery but it is hard to believe how much progress is being made when you feel and look like a pile of crap.

Janet's journal entry December 23rd:

David had a blood transfusion this morning. This is about the 6 one since his surgery. Besides the urinary catheter he still has the external pacemaker and one chest tube in place. All of the other tubes and IV's have been removed. They put a pic line in his upper arm today so that it would be easier to administer his daily antibiotic infusions without having to re-stick him each day. He was out of bed twice today and able with assistance to shuffle with a walker to the bedside chair.

Christmas came and went just as most of the early winter season without being outside. I did not see the downtown holiday lights, horse drawn carriages, or hustle and bustle of the holiday season. Frankly, I was not thinking about it that at the time. Janet along with my sister and brother-in-law were there at my bedside every day. I had visits from our minister, Reverend Colleen, as well as our son, daughter-in-law and grandsons and friends alike. Having the company definitely helped to lift my spirits. Our friends Bob & Teri made me banana bread which I cherished as it was some of the only palatable food I had. Janet brought me Subway tuna sandwiches on occasion making me very happy. The hospital food was horrible. Part of it may have been my deadened taste buds and my loss of appetite. Sleeping was a challenge because in addition to the bed being uncomfortable, my inability to move on my own and nurses coming into my room throughout the night to adjust my position, check my vitals, draw blood for tests and other medically related and personal hygiene issues. I was being moved from bed to chair where I spent many hours sitting with my legs elevated. I had air boots on my feet and legs that electronically created stimulation to prevent blood clots.

Janet's journal entry December 28th:

David still has one chest tube which will hopefully come out tomorrow. Still has the catheter. Plans are to release him to the rehab center tomorrow.

The heart surgeon's team was emphatic about me getting up, with assistance, many times a day and attempting to walk with the aid of a walker. I was able to move from my bed into the hall, about fifty steps. It was difficult as my legs felt like heavy torpedoes. I did not get breathless or have any pain, just extremely tired and weak.

Well, it is finally D-day, December 29th and I am being transferred to Heartland Rehab Center. My day started with a little excitement. Janet came to the hospital after breakfast to help get me dressed and ready to roll out. An ambulance was going to transfer me to the rehab center. My catheter was removed and my urine output was monitored by sonography. The guideline was I needed to empty my bladder to less than 300ml on my own. After the first test I was doing fine, within limits. On the second test, I was at 325ml and the nurse said they would have to straight cath me to fully empty my bladder. I was freaking out but did not have much choice in the matter. What transpired was misery on all accounts. The nurse brought the straight catheter kit into my room and got me prepped. One attempt – she could not thread the catheter, second attempt - no go. Now I was bleeding and she thought it best to have another nurse try. Second nurse made one attempt with no success and the mission was scrubbed. Here I am sore, bleeding and really upset. They called for a urology consult. A urology PA came to my room, made a medical assessment and said she would have to reinsert the urinary catheter leaving it there for at least a week until I healed from the debauchery. She very professionally inserted the catheter without difficulty. I was now ready to get the hell out of Dodge.

While this trauma was going on Janet was packing up all of the plants, cards and gifts sent and brought to me by many wonderful people. The transport finally arrived and I was bundled up with blankets and stuffed into a wheelchair. I was on my way. I remember that it was bitterly cold that day. The ride from Meijer Heart to the rehab center was about fifteen minutes. It was the first time I had been outside since my initial transfer from Saint Mary's Hospital to Meijer Heart Center back on

December 6th. Wow did it feel great to breathe outside air and see the streets covered in snow. I felt alive again being exposed to the environment.

Heartland Rehab Center

It's December 29th, a cold overcast day and I was in a medical transport being shuttled from Meijer Heart to Heartland Rehab in Grand Rapids. I am secured in a wheelchair, covered in blankets and belted to the chassis of the transport van. The driver is conversational and makes the ride pleasant as he navigates through the snow covered streets. I am excited to be leaving the hospital and getting ready to start a new chapter in my recovery. We arrive at the rehab center and the driver wheels me into the facility. It appears that they expected me as my room has already been assigned. Janet is going to meet me there after she drops all of the plants and things that were in my room at the heart center at our home. By the time I get to my assigned room Janet shows up and the admission process begins. An aid, the administrator and a nurse are all in my room. They take a complete inventory of my clothes and everything else that Janet has brought for me. I am given a list of rules along with information on my physical and occupational therapy as well as information on ordering my meals. After the nurse checks my blood pressure and pulse I am stripped out of my clothes so that a visual examination of my body can be made. They document every scar and mark on my body. The reason they do that is so that they have a record of what I looked like upon admission. Once all of that was completed and necessary paperwork was completed and signed I was given a tour of the facility. The place was broken up into sections depending on what a person was there for. My unit was a mixed bag of recovering surgical, stroke and trauma patients. They also have an Alzheimer's locked unit, a long term skilled nursing care unit and a permanent living area. After the tour I am wheeled back to my room. Not being able to walk I am confined to my wheelchair. Because of my open heart surgery, I am not allowed to use my arms to roll the chair so unless I have someone to push me I am stuck where my wheelchair is positioned. Janet stays for several hours comforting me as another wave of depression soon hits me along with tears and concerns. I have visions of slow or no progress before I even get started. I have my first dinner served in my room. I had the option of eating in my room, alone unless Janet or other company were there, or going to a dining area. Not feeling too social I elected to eat in my room which is where I ate for the three weeks I was there...breakfast, lunch and dinner. The food for the most part was not bad. It was certainly more palatable than the heart center. I have a pic line so that IV antibiotic can be administered two times a day. Each bag drips for one hour.

My first night at the rehab center they did not hang the bag until almost midnight so I was up until 1am. Between that and waking me a few times during the night to reposition me in the bed I did not get much sleep. Also the mattress felt like it was made out of a piece of drywall. I was getting Heparin shots in my stomach three times a day to keep me from developing clots due to my immobility. One of the injections was at 5 am. Vitals and weight were checked at 6 am so with all the waking, checking and crappy mattress how much sleep is a person getting, not much. With the long New Year's weekend, I did not start physical and occupational therapy for a few days. Other than sit in my wheelchair, look out the window and wait for Janet to come to be with me there was not much to do. The center had a list of things going on each day for the patients but not being a bingo player or into making bead projects there was not much for me to do. The patient population in my unit did not appear particularly conversational and not being ambulatory I was isolated. Other than the aids, nurses and therapists there was no one there to talk to. In short order I told Janet I was losing my mind. When Janet or other visitors were not there, I felt cooped up and alone. This did not change for the next three weeks. The only time I was occupied was when I had therapy, forty-five minutes for physical therapy and forty-five minutes for occupational therapy once per day five days a week. Well you might ask, what do you do the rest of the day? Answer. Nothing. I was getting a little nuts from boredom.

I finally started my therapy sessions on January 4th. When I began I was able to walk only a short distance with a walker. My first therapy visit was a complete evaluation of my status with the physical and occupational therapists. It was determined that physically I had lost most of my core strength and not being able to use my arms for support, I could not get up from a sitting position. Goal number one was to improve my core strength with a series of exercises designed for that purpose. The occupational therapist was going to work on strengthening my grip and helping to alleviate the severe pain and burning in my hands and wrists. I could tell from the start that the therapy was going to be of great help to me. At first it was hard and I became exhausted quickly. I had some frustration because I was not moving forward as quickly as I would have liked to. Everyone keeps telling me that it would take time for me to see the kind of improvement I desired but I was determined to walk again. Having a lot of time on my hands I would sit and think about my future and associated scenarios. I found myself focusing on and envying people that were able to walk. We take so much of that for granted until it is taken away. As the days progressed so did I. I found that in relatively short order I was walking, with assistance, the corridors outside my room. My legs continued to feel and look like stovepipes due to swelling from water retention. I was still on Lasix to help get rid of the excess fluid from my legs and body. I still had my catheter in place so peeing was a simple process. I still needed assistance toileting, dressing and undressing. Just as when I was in the hospital my vanity was nonexistent. I really could care less about having myself exposed and others tending to my body...it was the way it was and I dealt with it pretty well, I think.

My first real shower was heaven on earth. From the day of my first admission to the ER at Saint Mary's Hospital back in the beginning of December until now the only water cleaning my body were sponge baths given to me by the hospital aids. At Heartland Rehab I was scheduled three times a week for a shower. When they notified me that I was going for a shower the first time I felt like a kid in a candy store. I was wheeled into the shower room, stripped of my clothes, transferred to a shower chair where the aid lathered me up, scrubbed by back (that felt amazing), washed my hair, dried me and got me dressed. This was the most fantastic experience I had had since my first hospital admission. I called Janet to let he know and was almost crying with joy telling her about this mind blowing experience. I felt clean and relaxed.

I had a number of strange experiences while at Heartland. One of the best was one morning in my wheelchair. After breakfast one of the aids wheeled me to the sink so I could shave and brush my teeth after I got washed up and dressed. The sink was in a countertop with an open area beneath exposing the water supply pipes and drain with an "S" trap. There was very limited space between the sink and the wall so it made it difficult to turn the chair around. I somehow managed to hook the foot rests around the drain pipe under the sink. I was completely stuck and could not get the wheelchair loose no matter how hard I tried. What's more is that I was not in reach of my call button. With the door closed I was S.O.L. I called out several times but no one came to my rescue. Well, about forty-five minutes later one of the aids came to my room to check on me and was not able to open the door because my stuck wheelchair was blocking access. She managed to get into the room and after some maneuvering was able to free my wheelchair from the pipe. That was my excitement for the day which should give you an idea of how exciting my days were.

I was making great progress with my physical therapy and slowly gaining back strength allowing me to stand up without using my hands for support. I was gradually walking more and more with the help of a walker. One day, on the way back to my room from the therapy gym, the therapist asked if I wanted to try and walk without the aid of the walker. I agreed to try. She had a safety belt attached around my waist so that if I started to fall she could grab me. I let go of the walker and stood still for a few seconds and then took my first step. I walked very slowly for about thirty feet. It was scary and exhilarating at the same time. The first time I walked on my own brought tears to my eyes and a huge smile on my face. My greatest fear of not being able to walk again was no longer burnt into my mind. I had crossed the threshold and was on my way to the next level in my recovery. I worked hard every day taking the therapy seriously knowing that I could and would do it. My occupational therapy was coming along as well. The combination of the systemic infection, arthritis, Raynaud's, and Carpal Tunnel had wreaked havoc on my ability to use my hands for writing, using utensils to eat and pretty much anything else that required digital dexterity. The occupational therapist asked me what activity using my hands was necessary to me. I told her that I loved to cook and obviously needed use of my hands to do that. She asked me, as part of my therapy, if I would make dinner for her in the facility's kitchen one night. I prepared a shopping list of the ingredients I would need to put together a vegetarian meal for her. The next day she brought me into the kitchen, told me where all of the utensils, food and spices were to accomplish the cooking session. I felt terrific having the opportunity to show her and myself that I could cook up a great meal. I ditched my walker and proceeded to take command of the kitchen. It smelled so good that staff kept popping into the kitchen to see what was going on. Mission complete, she had a thumbs up meal and I took another step in the positive direction of my recovery.

As the weeks went by, I was continuing to feel extremely confined and bored. Unless I was in therapy or had Janet or guests I had no one to talk to and nothing to do. I wanted to go home and felt that I was ready. Janet and I had a meeting with the centers administration and a social worker. We set a discharge date and were in the process of arranging for physical and occupational therapy to continue after I was discharged. Our daughter-in-law is a DPT (Doctor of Physical Therapy) and she and Janet wanted to make sure that I was going to be able to navigate the stairs in our house before I came home permanently. One Saturday Janet took me home to see what I could do. I arrived home for the first time in several months and made my first attempt to navigate two levels of stairs. I made it upstairs, a little worn out but I made it. Another stride forward. When I got into our bedroom upstairs I laid down on our bed and almost melted away. Comfort at last, what a great feeling. We spent most of the day at our house with our son, daughter-in-law and two grandsons. We talked, I played some games with our older grandson and just absorbed being home.

I must say, it was a little strange. I was like a stranger in a strange land but I knew I would get used to it in very short order. At the end of the day I had to return to the rehab center and remain there until my discharge date. Having to go back was painful.

January 20th, was my discharge day from Heartland. I was all packed up, breakfast in my stomach, dressed and ready to get out of there. Janet picked me up, it was time to go. There was lots of snow on the ground but I had my boots on and my new walker ready as I was whisked away. Janet and I went to lunch and I beamed from ear to ear as a free man ready to begin the next chapter in my adventure. After a week of settling in at home we visited my infectious disease specialist and cardiac thoracic surgeon for medical release from their service. I also had appointments with my new cardiologist and primary care physician. All looked good medically. I was now no longer using the walker and just relying on a cane for support. I started and ended my occupational and physical therapy sessions within two months, ditched my cane and in was then in cardiac rehab.

Moving Forward

I survived my "Game Changer" and although I do not know how much more mental and physical capacity I will gain back I am determined to keep moving forward in a positive direction. Having been given a second chance at life with hopes of continuing my loving relationship with my soul mate, children, grandchildren, family and dear friends is the greatest gift and blessing I could have. I am not sure what divine plan if there is one has been set for me but I will keep searching in hopes of discovering my destiny. It is that driving forces that keeps me moving forward. As time goes forward I have noticed that my recollection and memory of what transpired seems to be growing dimmer. I am now noticing changes related to cognitive skills, memory and a general flat mental feeling which is with me a good portion of the time. I am not sure if it is from the stoke, the anesthesia and or being on the heart/lung machine that is responsible but I plan on seeking consultation to hopefully continue my recovery. This whole experience was so surreal. I could not have imagined that this could happen to me in a million years. It is still hard for me to wrap my head around this game-changing event. Most of us take so many of life's gifts and simple functions of for granted. Sometimes it takes a catastrophic event to strike the blow that makes us think about our mortality. For me, I was shaken to the core beyond anything I could have perceived. I was so close to losing my life and leaving it all behind. It's a reality that is hard to speak of and even put to paper. How can that not change one's perspective on life. There is nothing that can rival a near-death experience. The Game Changer, I have lived it and am living it but I am determined to learn from it and move forward without letting it consume my existence. As my life continues to move forward I will try to let this event fade into the endless abyss of time, never forgetting what I have learned from it.

David M Rothbart is a photographic artist and author. He spent many years working as a building consultant, environmental professional and a certified reserve specialist. He enjoys and is satisfied delving into his photographic art and writing. David loves spending time with his wife, family, grandchildren and friends. He is an avid traveler and has a keen appreciation and knowledge of wine. Having a new lease on life has opened up his appreciation of what is important and creates happiness. David realizes after his near death experience, his game changer, and the long recovery process that is still going on that life is to be lived and enjoyed with family and friends who he loves making his experience on this planet a meaningful and rewarding journey not to be taken for granted.

'Life is for the living   Death is for the dead

Let life be like music   And death a note unsaid.'

Langston Hughes

Made in the USA
Middletown, DE
16 August 2022

71537828R00024